A Little Bo
Climate Change

REVISED EDITION

by
Tom Wallace

A Little Book about Climate Change

Other books by Tom Wallace:

Conatus

Twenty-One Levels of Self-Deception

Three Miles of Rice Pudding

Utopia Governance and the Commons

Wild Body Wild Nature

Tales from a Distant Shore

Dreamtree

Another Pudding is Possible

Table of Contents

Introduction

We are used to hearing about the terrible things that may happen as a result of climate change — indeed, 'climate change' has morphed into 'the climate emergency' and even, 'the climate crisis'. The media seem almost to relish the reporting of all the bad news and the difficulties that may lie ahead. The iconic image is of a polar bear apparently stranded on a small ice flow, unwilling or unable to swim to safety. This book looks at the challenges that face us and then at possible solutions — focusing in particular on some ideas that do not get a lot of attention in other books or in the media.

The Challenges

The challenges which face us can be broadly grouped under three headings:

1. Global warming leading to climate change. This is mainly as a result of the burning of fossil fuels. Another factor is our agricultural practices (especially, ploughing and meat and dairy production). Also, there are feed-back loops from other environmental changes, such as warming temperatures leading to melting permafrost, which in turn leads to Methane (a

very potent greenhouse gas) escaping into the atmosphere.

2. Over-use of finite resources. In particular, 'peak oil' — meaning that the supply of oil and eventually other fossil fuels will reach a maximum production level and then inevitably supplies will start to run out. What remains before it is all gone will become more and more difficult to access, process and use. (We should note however that exploitation of non-conventional oil reserves — such as via fracking — offers a greatly expanded reserve of fossil fuel. There may be as much as 1,400 times that of conventional resources — although very much more difficult to exploit.)

3. Loss of bio-diversity and loss of habitat for other species as a result of human activities and the expansion of human territory.

Meeting the Challenges

Here are four broad ways that the above challenges could be met:

1. We take action to prevent further climate change so far as possible (mitigation) and to coping with crises already taking place (adaptation).

2. We work towards a smooth and peaceful transition from oil-based economies to ones based on alternative energy and fuel sources.

3. We re-evaluate our relationship with the rest of nature — perhaps giving back areas of land to return to wilderness as well as assessing the

rights of other species with whom we share this planet.

4. We seek to re-evaluate our attitudes with regard to the environment, money and economic growth and to awaken to ways in which our well-being might be understood and realised in other ways. The link between increased consumption (realised through economic growth) and human flourishing might come to be seen as a deeply flawed view of what makes a good society.

Perhaps it is clear that the first two solutions to our challenges — whilst daunting — could nevertheless be viewed as purely technical solutions. It is where many stop, hoping that a Western economic model of growth can be prolonged indefinitely into the future by ongoing technical fixes.

The technical fixes that are available right now are potentially more than sufficient to meet the challenge of climate change. However, the will to implement these fixes and the manner in which they may be implemented depends very much on the motivation for making the changes. Is it to secure an ever-increasing level of material wealth? Or do we recognise new goals and aspirations as individuals, communities and societies?

The challenges of the over-use of natural resources and the loss of bio-diversity are less amenable to purely technical solutions. And that's where the third and fourth solutions come into play. We need broader perspectives if we are to meet all our challenges.

We are still very much addicted to stuff as individuals, and societies see material prosperity as what constitutes 'the good life'. So we might solve the climate change problem, but at the expense of still using vast amounts of the Earth's natural resources and taking more and more land away from natural habitats. That might lead to a 'sustainable' world for humans, but if we destroy most of nature in the process, then is it a world we would really like to live in, or to leave to future generations? Sometimes this is called 'business as usual' but without the carbon. It's not really clear whether this is possible or if it would mean a whole lot of additional technical fixes needing to be brought in to make up for the diminishing world of nature.

Hence, there is more to be considered. How do we meet the challenge of climate change without an excessive reliance on technology? How do we manage our use of natural resources and our other impacts on nature such that all of nature can flourish and not just us humans? These are the questions this book tries to address.

I should say right at the outset that I think we have a future. I am not of the opinion that civilisation will collapse, or indeed, that the whole planet will suffer some kind of 'heat death' through runaway climate change. A century from now we may well have different worries from the ones I have described above. There may be political tensions between the Earth and Mars, problems with animal and plant species that have been 'resurrected' from their

DNA and questions over the legal rights of artificial intelligence. Humans will go on changing, inventing and exploring, so there will always be new challenges and looming catastrophes. But the point is, things get solved and we move on.

That's not to say that the current issues are not serious. One of the main concerns of climate change is that we reach a point where the rise in temperature caused by humans pushes nature to the point where further warming occurs because of nature herself, irrespective of what we might do. We'll look at this a bit more in the chapters ahead.

There has certainly been a ramping up of concern over climate change in the last few years, such that it is difficult for governments to ignore public feeling that something must be done. Targets have been set across much of the world. If fully implemented, we would be within a range of 1.5 to 2 degrees centigrade of extra warming (above pre-industrial levels) by 2100 — the target set by the Paris Climate Agreement of 2015.

An important split can be identified between solutions that try to reduce or stop the change and those that accept change is going to happen. The first types of solution are described as 'mitigation'. The second type of solution — living with the changes — is described as 'adaptation'. We'll look at each of these in turn over the following chapters.

Mitigation

This chapter and the next are looking mainly at climate change — the first of the challenges that we identified in the Introduction. As mentioned, there are two broad approaches to tackling climate change — mitigation and adaptation. Mitigation means to stop or reverse climate change, by whatever means. Adaptation, by contrast, is to accept that change is happening and to change our ways in turn so that we live with how the world is now and is likely to be in the future.

Because our climate is already changing there is inevitably going to be a bit of both mitigation and adaptation in whatever we choose to do. Looking at mitigation versus adaptation, something else is clear. Mitigation is a choice, but we may be forced to adapt! We might adapt well or we might adapt badly, but either way, it's not a choice. There are a few sceptics who suggest that we are already beyond a tipping point such that we are now unable to stop climate change from happening. Those feedback loops in nature (such as the sun's heat being absorbed more effectively by water than by ice and the release of Methane from thawing permafrost) are driving climate change forward no matter what we might choose to do. So, they conclude, it is mainly about adaptation. But, for now at least, many still believe that there is an opportunity to slow down or stop climate change, so mitigation measures are still important.

Both mitigation and adaptation aim at achieving sustainability. Sustainability has been defined as '....in a broad sense...the capacity to endure. It can be defined as the ability of an ecosystem to maintain ecological processes, functions, biodiversity and productivity into the future. In Biology, the word describes how biological systems remain viable and productive over time. For humans it is the potential for long-term maintenance of well-being, which in turn depends on the well-being of the natural world and the responsible use of resources.'

It also helps to distinguish between sustainability and 'sustainable development'. Jonathan Porritt, in *Capitalism as if the World Matters*, contrasts these two terms:

'Sustainability may best be defined as the *capacity for continuance into the long-term future*. Anything that can go on being done on an indefinite basis is sustainable. In that respect, capacity is the end goal, or desired destination, for the human species as much as for any other species.
'By contrast, sustainable development is the process by which we move towards sustainability ... sustainable development is a dynamic process which enables all people to realise their potential and to improve their quality of life in ways that simultaneously

protect and enhance the Earth's life-support systems.' (Author's emphasis.)

The phrase, 'sustainable development' is often used by politicians and others — perhaps trying to give the impression that we can still try to promote business whilst at the same time addressing climate change. But sometimes the phrase slides away from what Porrit was explaining above, into something more like: How can we keep on having economic growth without trashing the planet? So, it slides into contradiction, according to some folk. They would say that all resources are essentially finite and that therefore continual growth in a finite world is impossible. We would be well advised to heed the words of Kenneth E. Boulding, who says: 'Anyone who believes that exponential growth can go on forever in a finite world is either a madman or an economist.'

Who Should Change?

This brings us to the awkward question of who should be responsible for making the changes that mitigation is asking of us. Let's consider three options: government, the 'producer' (that is, agriculture and industry, especially large-scale industry) and the 'consumer'. We'll consider each of these in turn.

Government could just legislate climate change out of existence right now. Problem solved! To do this they might, for instance, ban the use of fossil fuels. Along with that, they might impose heavy penalties on all forms of pollution. And they might put large areas of the land and the ocean into protected zones where all exploitation of natural resources is forbidden, or strictly limited. Obviously though, such measures would put many millions of people out of work, cause economic meltdown and no doubt lead to civil unrest, if not world war! More to the point, any government suggesting such immediate and drastic change would likely be thrown out of office by its electorate (if the nation is a democracy) or face civil war in the more autocratic nations of the world. In other words, one way or another, it's us, the populations of each nation of the world, who determine how far any government can go in legislating for change.

So what about changing agriculture and industry? Well, both farmers and manufacturers must work within the constraints imposed by government, and as I've said above, if those constraints are too tough then there will be economic meltdown, the farm or the business will cease trading (or be forced to break the rules). Farmers and manufacturers need a market for what they produce. So again it is consumers who call the shots here.

That leaves us consumers. Can we make the change? Granted, sometimes businesses will try to create a market for products that we neither need or really want, by advertising and suggesting to us that we are not fully happy with our lifestyle, our homes, or our bodies until we have whatever it is they are trying to sell us. This, and similar arguments, imply that as consumers we are the passive victims of such manipulations by industry. But I think this is a cop-out. I think we can take responsibility for what we purchase, how we live and how we

14

work. For now, we can note that most of us are not politicians, most of us are not in a position to directly decide what farms grow and what businesses produce. But all of us are consumers. As such, we have the power to force change in society through our choices. So, whilst it might be a contentious point for some, I come down firmly on the side that says it is individual choice that is going to make the difference.

What Mitigation Means

There are a lot of books that explore the various means of mitigating climate change. I am giving just a brief summary here, and also focusing on a few things that get less of a mention but which impact very much on the above conclusion — that it is our own individual change that will drive the wider change in society. I group the mitigation measures under energy, buildings, transport, agriculture, forests, oceans and infrastructure and deal with each one of these below.

Energy

Energy is often the topic most familiar to us in any discussion on climate change. A lot of our energy still comes from fossil fuels. Burning these produces Carbon Dioxide and this builds up in the atmosphere and causes global warming. What's more, fossil fuels are running out, so even without the problems of climate change, we still need to be looking at alternatives over the long-term. The good news here is that the development of renewable energy is well under way and it is mostly cheaper than fossil fuels. So the change has gathered its own momentum and the days are numbered for the older power-generation industries.

Let's touch a little on the individual's involvement in all this, since that is the theme I'm seeking to emphasise throughout this book. The first thing to say, when we are looking at providing heating, hot water and power to our homes, is that electricity is always going to be the better option, so far as the planet is concerned. Even if the reader is living in a country where, for the moment, most energy is produced via the burning of fossil fuels, that is likely to change in the near future. Electricity will become increasingly based on renewable sources — increasingly green.

The other thing to consider is whether the household is getting its electricity from the nation's power grid, or if some or all of the energy is provided by the use of 'micro-renewables', such as solar panels, a small wind turbine or a micro-hydro scheme. If a household provides all of its own energy this is often referred to as being 'off-grid'. So we could ask here, is being off-grid worth it? Is it cheaper and is it better for the planet? We'll return to these questions below.

One thing to note is that if the home is relying solely on grid electricity for all its energy needs then it has a problem if there is a power cut. (Many gas- and oil-fired boilers also still need an electricity supply to function.) So it is a good idea to have some back up, at least for heating, and especially in a cold climate. A wood-burning stove is a good option here. (The jury is out on whether burning wood is a positive or a negative for the planet. For the UK at least, our land area to population size would only allow about a tenth of households to burn wood before we'd need to start importing and then this option tips towards a negative impact on climate over all.)

The next point is that, yes, solar power and such things as ground- and air-source heat pumps (which deliver more heat for a given amount of energy input) will eventually pay for themselves and energy bills will be cheaper. The caveat here is how long will these products last? And the further caveat is to ask: Is it more difficult and expensive over all to have every household fitted with such devices, or would it be better to put all our efforts into a more environmentally-friendly grid system?

Along with that, there may be opportunities for district energy and heating schemes that work out cheaper and more efficient than fitting out individual houses. There could, for instance, be a large wind turbine that provides electricity to a village. Or there may be a large heat pump that takes energy from something like a lake or an underground aquifer and delivers the heat to homes at a lower cost than if each home had an individual pump.

Of course, for most of us, our choices are limited, so switching to having a home which is all-electric is probably the most significant thing we could do. There is nevertheless the lure of independence from the big energy providers that micro-renewables can offer us. We asked earlier if going off-grid is worthwhile financially and for the planet. We can say that, for one thing, it is a lifestyle decision that moves people towards self-reliance. That appeals to a lot of people. It is not necessarily a simpler lifestyle. The kit might be quite complex. Even if the choice were to keep things as simple as possible, with just a stove for heating and cooking, candles for lighting and batteries for a few household gadgets, the householder still needs to think about keeping a supply of all their energy and lighting sources, for all weathers, etc. So if we are really serious about off-grid, then we need to set aside a lot of time to collect wood, light the stove, heat water and cook meals and maintain a supply of candles and batteries. Could we all live off-grid? For the UK, as we saw above, there is not enough local timber to allow wood to be part of an off-grid solution for more than about a tenth of households. If we were not to use so much timber, then being off-grid would mean relying on more technical solutions such as solar panels. (No doubt what I've said above about a stove, candles and batteries sounds horrific, so this is probably the more favoured version of off-grid!) All that would really achieve would be to move the complexities of energy supply, demand, and necessary infrastructure around quite drastically, but probably not making us more sustainable over all.

Short of going off-grid, I think it's best to go for a 'normal' house, but with as much insulation and draft-proofing as we can pack in. Put shutters on the windows and heavy curtains to reach the floor. Have carpets rather than bare floorboards. I posed the question above of whether the more technical micro-renewable installations are really worthwhile over all, compared to say, a better national electric grid. In balance, I worry about how effective micro-renewables such as heat pumps and solar panels will be long-term for an individual house. So I suggest don't bother with hi-tech 'renewable' gizmos. Use stand-alone electric heaters and a power shower. If the household is willing to put up with a bit of inconvenience, just boil a kettle to get hot water for washing dishes etc. Otherwise, have a small instant electric water heater, easily accessible, on each hot water tap. Install a wood-burning stove with a hot plate, to allow one room to be heated and water to be boiled (and a simple meal to be prepared) in the event of a power cut.

Buildings

When we turn to buildings themselves, there are a few general questions we can ask and then again we can focus in on the small-scale individual householder.

The first thing to look at is cities. More than 50% of humans live in cities and the proportion is rising. Is this a good idea, from the planet's point of view? In favour of cities, they leave more space elsewhere for nature to thrive. They make transport and infrastructure easier to provide (as long as people generally stay in their own city and are not continually travelling across the globe). Cities tend to promote innovation amongst people for technology and the arts. They allow specialist businesses to thrive because there is a sufficient base of local population to provide them with adequate revenue. On the negative side of cities: storm events and heat waves hitting cities cause intensified devastation. There is a disconnect from nature. There may be problems supplying the food, water and energy requirements to people when we are clustered in high densities. There is an atomising and alienating effect from cities and it can be difficult to achieve good neighbourhoods and communities when people do not feel any kind of cultural or social connection with where they live.

So do cities come out better or worse for the planet? It is a personal view, and not backed up by any research, but I think there is a threshold beyond which the problems of alienation mentioned above outweigh the advantages of cities. Somehow we seem to want some kind of local connection, but once cities get beyond a few million in population this seems to be difficult to achieve. Bureaucracy cannot cope with the mega-city.

Next we can ask about the scale of buildings within our towns and cities. Here again there is a balance to be struck. The taller the building the more likely it is that it will rely on technology to be built and to function. A tall building mostly needs to be of steel (although there are some timber skyscrapers) and it will need a lot more in the way of infrastructure for lifts, fire protection, water supply, and so on. The plus side of tall buildings however is that more funds can be raised from the sale or rent of a property which is a high-rise building than a building of lower height. Indeed, there are places where low-rise buildings may be unviable, from a financial point of view. So, is there a cut-off point? Probably yes, around eight storeys as a maximum. The financial issues raised above are certainly pertinent though. I think the wider question of the way we treat land is the issue here. The tall height of buildings is a symptom of things being wrong in the economics around land use. So to get to smaller and more compact cities we would have to address the politics around owning, buying and selling land, as a first step. This, of course, is outwith the scope of the consumer, so I leave the question aside.

We have touched on building materials above and we can go on to ask about materials more generally and to focus in on matters that effect the individual householder.

We could generalise here by saying that the more natural the materials, the better. But this comes with a few caveats. Natural materials may be scarce and expensive in a particular location and the householder may struggle to afford them. Also, natural materials may require greater skill, time and expense in terms of construction and future maintenance. So once again there is a balance to be struck.

Smaller buildings are obviously cheaper all round and buildings closer to cubes are more energy-efficient than sprawling buildings that have a high surface area compared to their volume. A flat or a terraced house — all things being equal — is going to be more energy-efficient than a detached building of the same volume.

Large areas of glazing and external doors are

especially wasteful of energy in colder climates (although south-facing windows can provide some heat from solar gain). Even the best triple glazing is only about one tenth as good as the equivalent area of well-insulated wall.

It always pays to insulate! Provided the insulation is well fitted and there is adequate ventilation to each construction element, then insulation is always a worthwhile investment.

There are some oddities that come up when we think about the costs of buildings and their materials and fittings. Take, for instance, the fitted hob and fitted oven — now more or less standard features of a kitchen in the Western world. Look at the prices of these and compare them with stand-alone hobs and ovens. Perhaps they are around ten times the cost. And how about comparing an oil-filled radiator fitted to a wall with one that is just stand-alone and plugged into a wall socket? Again, several times the price for what is essentially the same thing. Returning to windows, look at the cost of a sheet of glass (or even the cost of a double-glazed unit bought separately from a window) and then the cost of a complete window with the same area of glass. Almost certainly a huge difference in price and yet the window frames are usually made from relatively cheap materials. The DIY enthusiast could probably put together some simple window frames with shutters and draught excluders, with the glass bought separately and have something nearly as energy-efficient as a manufactured window, but at a fraction of the cost. Many such examples could be given for buildings and we will see a similar pattern for food later on.

The bizarre point is that business (and often governments as well) don't like us getting involved in DIY of any kind! Everything is sealed up, packaged and made difficult and costly to repair. Or it is made to seem more complex than it really is, just so that we can be dumbed down as consumers. Then we will just buy what is offered to us and throw things away when they break. Instead we could be making, inventing, re-using, and repairing for ourselves and for our neighbours.

Transport

Thus far, there is something of a pattern that can be identified in the various alternatives that might help us in our efforts to mitigate climate change. The pattern is this. If we can replace something that is causing a problem for the climate with something equally good that does not cause a problem, then this is likely to be the kind of solution that people will accept. For instance, as long as the house is warm, the lights stay on and there is adequate hot water, we may not be too concerned with whether the energy for all this comes from fossil fuels or from renewables. The transition does not involve any sacrifice. Indeed, the transition may even save us money.

When it comes to transport however, we are on the edge of a bigger problem. From the above, we might take that same discussion about replacing something with 'equal and as good' but more environmentally-friendly and apply it to cars and other means of transport. So we could say, if an electric car gives the same level of comfort and convenience as the petrol car, then there is no sacrifice to be made — we have achieved that 'equal and as good' criterion and the planet has been helped into the bargain.

Also, transport takes us to the edge of those other challenges we met in the Introduction. Whilst we can have unlimited energy from nature and could build our homes entirely from natural products, if we chose, we cannot create a transport network without impacting on non-renewable resources and also impacting heavily on natural habitats.

As I write this in 2021, the UK, along with many Western nations, is already well under way towards the change to electric vehicles. As we've said above, this change, whilst substantial, is not one that is going to cause massive disruption to society. People's lifestyles are unaffected, just as a change to electric heating means little to folk as long as their house is warm. At face value, electric transport will be a huge step forwards in the effort to mitigate climate change, as the reliance on fossil fuels will be broken. But looked at in a broader context, is it all good?

For one thing, the massive infrastructure of roads, service stations and all the other ancillary industries related to transport will more or less remain intact. Apart from still having to build and maintaining the road network, a huge growth industry for electric batteries has to be created to sustain electric vehicles. These currently rely on fairly scarce resources for their manufacture. Then there are all the materials for the cars themselves, which will remain little changed when moving from petrol to electric. A lot of the air pollution caused by vehicles is from the wear on tyres and brakes, so this also remains a problem. Accidents and the disruption caused by roadworks and traffic jams remain. We'll be looking at infrastructure in more detail below, but for now it is worth bearing in mind that electric vehicles still remain problematic.

When we consider air travel this is when the impact on lifestyle really starts to hit home. Suggesting that we should give up or severely limit flying is where a lot of people start to switch off. The holiday is built into the Western lifestyle and many people take great pride in telling others about all of the trips they have made over their lifetime. The more exotic and remote their destinations, the better. These are collected like badges of honour.

If we try to encourage people to switch to public transport instead of using their private cars then we face similar difficulties. The autonomy and convenience of the car is just too much to give up, despite all the issues that will remain with us even after the change to electric vehicles.

What then can be done? One possible solution goes back to our earlier discussions on cities. This is where 'walkable' towns and neighbourhoods — such that all or most of the facilities we need in our day-to-day lives are available close to hand — come into their own. Another, and related, solution is to do a lot more to encourage community. With strong community, people will want to remain at home or close by, in case they should miss out on all the excitement happening on their own doorsteps! When the UK and many other nations locked down in the spring of 2020, because of the Covid 19 pandemic, we had a glimpse of what things could be like. Wildlife seemed to flourish and people went out walking, visiting their local parks and beauty spots and their local shops. Was that really such a bad life? Remember too that a similar move in response to climate change would not stop us from seeing friends and family — which of course was something we had to miss out on during the pandemic. We could do something similar to that Covid lockdown in response to climate change and reap the benefits of this as a permanent solution.

Agriculture

Agriculture is another area where there is potentially a big impact on the lives of individuals. For much of the thirty or forty years when the dangers of climate change have been understood, agriculture has been something of the forgotten element in comparison to our use of fossil fuels. But now it is widely recognised that a great deal of our agricultural land is given over to raising cattle and that this choice leads to problems. We could feed a lot more people with a lot less land if everyone were to adopt a largely vegetarian diet. On the other hand, a diet with a high meat content means a lot more wild nature destroyed to make way for cattle farming. This causes a huge strain on water resources and some very serious social justice issues as poorer nations struggle to feed their own populations whilst catering for the wealthier nations' obsession with beef and salmon.

These are complex issues of course and there are many instances of small-scale organic farms where animals and fish form important elements in very rich, balanced and sustainable methods of food production. Farming communities throughout the world will often see the concern for nature and calls for 're-wilding' as somewhat sentimental and very often promoted by urban middle-class folk with little knowledge of what rural living and food production really involve. I have some sympathy with this view, but nonetheless, without a viable natural world there would be no human world. In the 1960's, two thirds of the land area of the planet could be described as wild nature. Now, in the 2020's, it's down to less than one third. As we will see in the next sections, this is not a situation that can continue for much longer. In the meantime, agricultural practices such as permaculture (including ocean permaculture) and 're-generative' farming successfully mix animal husbandry, care for wild nature and food growing without the use of synthetic fertilisers and pesticides. And they still turn a profit! So, whilst every country and climate has its own unique circumstances, it seems there is great scope for agriculture everywhere to change for the better, giving us healthier diets and more space for nature.

But again, what about the consumer — what can we do? Western nations are obsessed with food, and suggesting to people that they should change their diets is therefore fraught with difficulties. It's fairly easy to say, don't fly, don't drive, as these are simple messages, albeit often unwelcome ones. But, just to say, 'don't eat meat' is not nearly as simple. Many food crops involve the destruction of wildlife habitats and pollution from pesticides and from the over-use of fertiliser. So we may save some animals but at the same time inadvertently kill a huge number more as a result. Also, many foods sold in the UK and other Western nations undergo a great deal of processing and packaging, which greatly adds to their impact on the environment, even when the food in question is vegetarian or vegan.

I can only offer two simple messages here. Go with what can be obtained locally, preferably from an organic farmer, even if that involves some meat, poultry or fish. And, cook from scratch, if possible. Similar to the household appliances we discussed above, it's amazing how much price gets added to food just from it being packaged and sold to us as a 'ready meal'.

Forests and Oceans

Like agriculture, forests and oceans have been something of the poor cousins when it came to looking at the concerns of climate change in the past. For one thing, living systems were often left out of early climate models. Forests and oceans affect the amount of water vapour in the atmosphere. Water vapour is itself a greenhouse gas, and it is also difficult to include in climate models, so also often gets left out. But now the importance of forests and oceans is much more clearly understood, both for our climate and for those other challenges we have in mind — the loss of natural resources and the decline in bio-diversity. Also — and something we do not hear discussed very much — the forests and oceans provide us with most of the Oxygen in our atmosphere. Without forests and marine organisms, the amount of Oxygen would decline. So a dead ocean or a flattened forest is not just a tragedy because, in balance, the forests and oceans absorb Carbon Dioxide and help mitigate climate change. Or even for the loss of wildlife such destruction represents. It is also a serious risk to the viability of all Oxygen-breathing creatures on the planet.

So, the protection of forests and oceans is not just about having these wild places around for us to enjoy, even although that is important. Nor is it just about all the resources that the forests and oceans provide us with, although clearly that is important too. It is a matter of life and death. Without viable living oceans and substantial forests there would be very little life able to survive on the planet. So, whilst there is a link between forests, oceans and climate change, they are also a major concern in their own right. Even if there were no climate change, the loss of forest and living oceans could more or less wipe us out.

I recognise that for many of us the preservation of forests and the health of the oceans are distant goals and ones that we probably feel powerless to affect. But there are some modest things we can do on our own doorstep that will support these efforts, at least in spirit. I am thinking of the preservation of local parks, trees, rivers, ponds and lakes close by to where we live. If we are fortunate enough to have a garden, hopefully it can be kept at least as lawn and flower beds and not covered over with tarmac or paving. Or why not grow some food?

I know these are small matters compared to the plight of the Amazon rainforest or the Great Barrier Reef, but in the spirit of this book, every individual decision matters.

Re-wilding, coupled with better agricultural practices, could make an enormous difference to the UK and to most countries across the world. It would take a lot of discussion and a lot of skilful negotiations, but could be a win for everyone if we were really serious about it. And, in terms of the planet, we still potentially have just enough time to make a very substantial contribution towards mitigating climate change, just through working in harmony with nature for the forests, the oceans and for food growing.

Infrastructure

'Economies of scale' is a term long since presented as a means by which large populations can benefit from goods and services that might otherwise be difficult and expensive to provide at a local level. Capitalism has embraced the term, and more or less taken it to be a given that manufacturing on a large scale and then distributing the products is always going to be more cost-affective. It means more profit for the manufacturer and cheaper goods and more choice for the consumer. Is this true? Well, from the manufacturer's (or service-provider's) point of view, usually, yes. And the reason it is true is mainly because of the infrastructures that are in place to allow for the economy of scale to happen. The infrastructure includes the electricity grid, water supply and drainage, gas supply, roads, railways, telephone, internet, wi-fi and airlines. Whilst, like all of us, businesses will be paying a contribution towards these things, they will by no means be paying the true cost. That money usually comes via the government, and therefore from taxation. Thus, ultimately, it is us consumers who are subsidising the costs. So it is not surprising that economies of scale seem to work so well. Most of the costs are hidden from us, and most of the costs are borne unwittingly by us, the customers. If we were to do the sums differently and tried to see the costs in terms of their impact on the climate, on resources and on nature, then a very different picture emerges. Now the scenario of centralised manufacturing and services with complex distribution systems appears as a very expensive and wasteful system. And that element that might seem the most benign, the wi-fi connectivity for all manner of communication and information exchange, is actually amongst the most harmful and wasteful of all.

Infrastructure then is one of the most hidden, least obvious issues that we face when tackling climate change. Much of the world has gone down this route of building up its infrastructure because it has genuinely appeared to be the right thing to do. So we have a very difficult task if we were to try to convince people that actually it makes life more expensive rather than cheaper and causes great harm to the planet into the bargain. We don't see this argument presented to us very often as a means of mitigating climate change — and that's not surprising, it seems counter-intuitive.

With so much investment in infrastructure, we might at least expect that things would be improving in terms of supply of goods and services. And that therefore it may be worth it, even if it is really us consumers who bear the brunt of the costs. But even this hope is increasingly precarious. The reliance on wi-fi and the internet is of particular concern. If there were a power cut at a local corner shop, they might not even be able to sell a loaf of bread, because their till is electronic and wi-fi connected. Our bank accounts are increasingly vulnerable to hackers and fraud and if the bank's computers go down then it means significant disruption for businesses and individuals.

Governments, meanwhile, seem intent on pushing for improvements to wi-fi, with the aim of keeping industries 'competitive'. An increasing proportion of defence budgets go towards cyber-security. The government (in the UK at least) does not generally encourage back-up plans, for when there are power cuts or wi-fi shut downs, or when there is a break in the supply chain for food and other essentials. (If backup plans were put in place then arguably this would be real defence and real security.) And businesses, even although they would be wise to put in place their own contingencies, either cannot afford to do so, or they just take the risk that they can sit out any problems that might come along.

All of this may seem a long way from our discussions about climate change, resources and bio-diversity. But as I've said above, with cyberspace in particular, we are talking about huge impacts. It may seem that the mobile phone and the laptop use tiny amounts of power, and this is true. They therefore seem rather innocent compared to trucks, aircraft and container ships. But we tend to forget — or, are just unaware of — the massive infrastructure behind our phones and computers and the enormous amounts of natural resource that go into manufacturing our high-tech gadgets. Generally speaking, the more complex the technology, the greater the infrastructure needed to support it (and often the more hidden and remote this is from us consumers). And let's face it, the world seems to have a voracious appetite for more technology — what it calls 'progress'.

Following the pattern I've established in the previous sections, we can ask, what can the individual do? And here, I have to say, I am a bit stumped for suggestions, as even the most dedicated off-gridder must rely, to some extent, on many of the infrastructures I have listed above. Short of becoming a hunter-gatherer, we are all forced into participating, unless society were to decide wholesale to abandon its commitment to distribution and instead promote local self-sufficiency and resilience. Such local autonomy is indeed promoted by such groups as the Transition Town movement, as a step towards being prepared for more extreme climate change and scarcity of resources. But I have to say that for now it is a tough choice.

I notice though that even those who have perhaps little knowledge of these matters seem nonetheless to have some kind of instinctive appreciation of them. Hence, the climate activist using a laptop or a mobile phone is seen as something of a contradiction.

You may have arguments to counter this (such that — and probably correctly — there's not really any escape from wi-fi). Or you may argue that, in balance, the greater connectivity afforded by these devices is worth it for the sake of trying to save the planet. But I think it's worth noting people's responses. Could the activist go without a mobile or a laptop?

I leave these thoughts with you and turn now to the second method of addressing climate change — adaptation.

Adaptation

The world may be very close to the point where mitigation measures are not enough to stop climate change. We noted earlier that as the temperature rises natural feedback loops come into play, causing more heat, even if we humans were to cut our emissions to zero. There may not be a stable climate at two degrees above pre-industrial levels. Two degrees of warming may force the temperature to go to three or four degrees before the planet settles into a new stable state.

In the previous chapter we looked at the familiar mitigation measures of cutting our use of fossil fuels and making changes in order to save energy. We also looked at less familiar measures, such as changes to agriculture, the preservation of our forests and oceans and re-considering our infrastructure. If we did all of these things, on a huge scale, and within a few years, then there is still a chance that we will avoid the runaway warming that I have described above. Even if we were successful, it would be many decades before there were signs of the planet beginning to cool. We would need to maintain our efforts for centuries in order to keep things in balance and return to something like the climate and natural environments we enjoyed as recently as the 1960's!

There are other options out there however, and I want to discuss these briefly before moving on to the more conventional adaptation measures that are the main subject of this chapter. In fact, the options discussed here might be considered as sitting somewhere between mitigation and adaptation. They can be grouped under the collective term, 'geo-engineering'.

Geo-engineering

I am just listing the various options here, without going into too much detail on each individual proposal. Here are the alternatives:

1. Stratospheric Sulphates. We currently try to reduce sulphates in the atmosphere, as they fall to Earth as acid rain. Sulphates that are higher up in the stratosphere would take longer to fall back to Earth and would reflect back sunlight so would cool the temperature within days. Tiny droplets of sulphuric acid have been proposed. One argument against this form of cooling is that — borrowing a phrase from economics — it is a moral hazard. The comparison is made with bailing out an organisation that has got itself into trouble because of risky business deals. To rescue such an organisation is seen as unhelpful in the long term as it sends a signal to others that similar risky dealings are okay because they can also be assured of a bail-out. So the comparison being made — the 'moral hazard' with regard to climate change — is that, effectively, we run the risk that people will take the cooling of the atmosphere to mean we can

continue burning fossil fuels with impunity. However, if the production of sulphates were ever stopped, then within a few days the temperature would revert to the 'real' temperature for however much Carbon Dioxide is in the atmosphere at that time — potentially with catastrophic consequences. Increased Carbon Dioxide also causes acidification of the oceans, risking even further harm to our already threatened marine habitats. Stratospheric sulphates do not solve this problem.

2. Ocean spray used to create increased cloud cover. The type of cloud produced is called Stratocumulus and already occurs naturally — mostly near the equator. Again, the intention is to reflect more sunlight back into space and thereby keep the temperature lower. (This still does not resolve increased Carbon Dioxide causing acidification of the oceans. And once again, if the process stopped for some reason, then temperatures would quickly escalate to their 'real' levels.)

3. Mirrors in space to reflect sunlight away from the Earth. The mirrors would be at the LaGrange point, where the Earth and the Sun's gravitational pull cancel each other out. (Also does not resolve increased CO_2 causing acidification of the oceans.)

4. 'Biochar'. Essentially charcoal buried as organic fertiliser, locking in large amounts of Carbon Dioxide. (This, and all subsequent measures, involve locking up Carbon Dioxide and therefore resolve the ocean acidification issue.)

5. Direct sequestration of Carbon Dioxide from the atmosphere and storage (possibly in the form of Magnesium Carbonate).

6. Increasing the iron content of marine

plankton so that they fix more Carbon Dioxide in the oceans.

7. Genetically engineering microbes that can absorb large quantities of Carbon Dioxide.

8. BECCS (Biomass with Carbon Capture and Storage). CCS technology is mostly envisaged for removing Carbon Dioxide from conventional fossil fuel plants. Combined with biomass however, it would effectively be a carbon neutral industry. Again however, the amount of land needed to supply the biomass would be colossal and would remove land from food growing.

9. Just plant trees! The problem is it would take around seven million square kilometres of new forest to sequester the extra Carbon Dioxide we currently add to the atmosphere. Nature's sequestration of Carbon Dioxide in other areas, such as the oceans, may slow as a result. One report suggests the net effect of the extra forest cover might be a 40ppm (parts per million) reduction in Carbon Dioxide. We touched on forests in the last chapter. We should distinguish between mass tree-planting and the preservation and protection of natural, especially old-growth, forests. A 'geo-engineering' approach to forestry would mean just trying to get the maximum carbon sequestered — maybe combined with industrial-style forest management. Alternatively (and perhaps more welcome) would be re-wilding of the landscape to heal and restore eco-systems. The latter might not produce such fast and profitable resources, but would be better in the longer-term.

What can we say about these various alternatives? For one thing, they mostly rely on a good deal of co-operation between nations.

One nation could not easily go it alone with most of these proposals. Remember that a few countries, such as Russia, Canada and Greenland, will probably have a net benefit from at least a modest rise in global temperatures. So agreement may be difficult. One country could however do some direct Carbon capture, or introduce 'biochar' into their agricultural systems, but unless it is a very large and wealthy nation, this is not going to make a lot of difference.

The second thing to say about the geo-engineering solutions is that, for the most part, they are massive technological projects, and therefore very expensive. The exception here is again biochar and also the first solution on the list, seeding the atmosphere with sulphates. (Possibly the cloud-seeding and the microbes are also cheap, but this is a bit uncertain for now.) The third comment to make is that all of the geo-engineering solutions are relatively quick fixes. If deployed at scale, they would bring global temperatures back down to pre-industrial levels within a matter of a few years, at most. If one or more of the solutions were ramped up to scale right now then the impact would coincide with the really dangerous time frame of around 2030, when it looks like we might be otherwise too late to avert very serious climate change impacts. We need, however, to introduce a few caveats here. For one thing, some of the proposed solutions, as indicated in the descriptions, do not actually remove Carbon Dioxide from the atmosphere, they only dampen the temperature. So Carbon Dioxide levels may go on rising in the background and this still causes problems, such as the acidification of the oceans — which could impact severely on marine eco-systems. Also, it means that whatever geo-engineering solution is put in place, it would have to continue into the indefinite future, unless of course we were to continue our more standard mitigation efforts, in which case we could gradually wean ourselves off the geo-engineering quick fix. This way, geo-engineering could be regarded as a way of buying time, but it should not be regarded as a permanent solution. (This would be the 'moral hazard' mentioned in point one of the list. Would we actually use the geo-engineering solutions just to buy time, or would we come to rely on them for the long-term?)

Finally, and perhaps the reason why we should treat geo-engineering solutions with a great deal of scepticism, the results are highly unpredictable. Conducting such large-scale experiments on the entire planet is an incredibly risky business, even if we tried smaller-scale experiments first. The exceptions again are biochar, direct Carbon capture and planting trees, all of which can be deployed in a piecemeal manner, and as I've discussed above, have the advantage of removing Carbon Dioxide from the atmosphere.

The world may one day be at a point where things are so bad that large-scale implementation of geo-engineering is the only option left to avoid total catastrophe. A small group of nations may then go it alone and roll out a quick fix, in a desperate attempt to bring temperatures down. In the meantime, out of all the solutions I've grouped together as geo-engineering, only direct Carbon capture, biochar and forestry come through as safe and relatively benign options. My concern though with Carbon capture is its reliance on technology. On a small-scale it works, but makes only a minor contribution at a significant cost. To deploy it at anything like the scale necessary to make an impact on global temperatures would involve so much industrial production it is doubtful whether the world economy could ever afford it. Of course that may change, but meanwhile it looks like biochar and forestry are the only real winners. These can be deployed as part of our efforts to improve agricultural practices, along with re-wilding as a way to help restore natural habitats. All of this can be tailored to different climates and different types of farming. It is relatively cheap and it seems not to have any undesirable side-effects.

We turn now to measures that can truly be described as adaptation and the first of these is to adapt to rising sea levels.

Sea-Level Rise

As I've said above, even if we manage to make drastic reductions in our Carbon emissions over the next few years, there will still be some further warming over the coming decades (short of deploying a geo-engineering quick fix) and hence some requirement for adaptation. And if we don't make radical change in the next few years then our adaptation measures will need to be very significant. There is general agreement that to mitigate would be very much cheaper than to adapt. But as these crucial years tick by it is looking increasingly likely that we will run out of time for mitigation and will be forced into more and more complex adaptation measures. Some governments have at least some plans in place. But for the most part, as with mitigation, it is too little, too late. Of course, governments are in the unenviable position of having to weigh up the odds of global mitigation measures being a success or a failure. If mitigation were globally successful, then much of the adaptation plans would be abortive. We can at least be sure that in many nations, insurance companies will in part shape what government fails to do.

And that brings us to our most pressing adaptation requirement — coping with sea-level rise.

As global temperatures increase then some sea-level rise occurs just because of the expansion of water. A little more is added by the melting of sea-ice, although not a great deal, as much of this is already more or less fully submerged. The vast majority of sea-level rise occurs because of the melting of ice that is on land — mainly the Greenland and Antarctic ice sheets. If all of the Greenland ice sheet were to melt this would raise global se-levels by several metres. If all the ice in the world were to melt then the rise would be about 70 metres.

So what kind of rise might be expected in the near future? Current estimates suggest a little over half a metre by 2100. However, with each year that passes, the predictions seem to increase. It used to be thought that it would take hundreds of years for Greenland or Antarctica's ice to fully melt, but as studies of ice have advanced, the possibilities of rapidly increased melting seem more likely. As a consequence, predictions for sea-level rise go up as well. What sort of temperatures would we need to reach before there is a possibility of all the ice melting? The Arctic, as a region, is heating up a lot faster than the rest of the planet, so Greenland's ice sheet is currently the main concern. But ice is melting at an increasing rate everywhere already, with our global average rise of 1.2 degrees Celsius. So, even if we only warmed to an average of two degrees, this would probably be enough to melt all the ice eventually. As I've said above, a two degree rise is not thought to produce a stable climatic state for the Earth, so if we reach two degrees we may well reach three or four. The melt and sea-level rise would be much, much faster.

Realistically then, preparing coastal towns and cities for half a metre or even a metre of sea-level rise is just putting off the inevitable and it is doubtful if any city could justify the flood defences for anything much more than this. There is only one choice and that is higher ground.

The reader, I am sure, will appreciate the dilemma for government. To move a large part (in some cases, all) of their population is a massive undertaking, and would take years to accomplish. Meanwhile, climate change may be stopped, and even reversed, so then a government's efforts to build on higher ground would be in vain. It is understandable therefore that the emphasis tends to be on flood defence. And of course, it is doubtful if any government could afford to save every town and village that lies on its coastline. The cities will be protected, but some places will be left to the waves (and hence the involvement of the insurance companies in the decisions around who will be helped and who will be abandoned). Those places abandoned can only hope for some compensation, to help householders and businesses to move by their own efforts. Make no mistake then, even if the government has no plans, the insurance companies certainly will.

In thinking about sea-level rise, we need to remember that it is not just the normal level of the water at high tide that is of concern. More deadly, by far, is the 'storm surge', when tides and wind direction conspire to push the sea much deeper into coastal regions. In warmer climes, low-lying coastal regions are protected from such onslaughts by mangrove forests and coral reefs. Not only do such features protect our shores, they also provide a haven for wildlife. However, warmer and more acidic oceans are putting our reefs at risk, whilst human development threatens the mangroves.

Extreme Weather

A similar story plays out when we consider another factor in climate change — the more extreme weather events that can cause flash floods and landslides. Again, nature comes to our aid here. Forested hillsides soak up rainfall and excess water gets slowed down, as it seeks lower ground. Meanwhile, the rivers and streams, if swollen by rainfall, find a natural overflow in flood plains and water meadows. Once again, all such places are havens for wildlife. Such natural flood defences could probably endure the kinds of intense rainfall that we are seeing more of as the planet warms. But of course, very often the trees on the hillsides have been cut down, the flood plains have become farmland or housing and the rivers have been dredged and forced between narrow concrete embankments or even channelled underground. Such rivers may be a useless trickle in the summer and a raging torrent in the winter. The wildlife has gone, and what was once both a joy and a resource for humans has become a threat to life and property.

So the message to the individual should be obvious here. Be careful where you choose to live! Remember that sewers and other infrastructures can become unviable long before water is actually seeping into homes and businesses. Unfortunately, governments are only coming around very slowly, if at all, to the notion that it is better to work with nature than against her in these matters. The natural defences that I have described above are not seen as good for economic development. Too often it seems that nature's silent protection is only appreciated once it is gone.

So when it comes to adaptation to sea-level rise and flooding, our concerns for climate change and for nature very much converge. Protecting and enhancing nature is both a means of mitigating the effects of climate change and a means to help us to adapt to its effects.

Flooding, Food Scarcity and Migration

As the climate changes, we face further extreme weather events that will require us to adapt.

Weather patterns and ocean currents are changing. Sometimes extreme cold can push down to very low latitudes. Sometimes heatwaves can set in, even in very northerly regions. Hurricanes and tornadoes are getting more intense. Severe drought may be interspersed with torrential downpours. Perhaps the biggest concern from all of these is the disruption to agriculture.

In the previous chapter we saw how alternative forms of agriculture could assist us in our efforts to mitigate climate change. Would such measures cope better than industrial farming with the extreme weather events I'm describing here? I think the answer is yes, up to a point. All types of farming are a battle with the weather, and there are limits to what could be done before food growing becomes so difficult and expensive it's just not viable. Nations, even quite wealthy ones, may not be in a position to import their food supply from elsewhere. As such, the only viable option may be migration. So, whilst sea-level rise, flooding and extreme weather events may be the direct cause of some migration (especially migration internally to nations) it is disruption to food supply that is likely to be the main driver.

I think large-scale migration is probably our biggest challenge in terms of adaptation. I'm sure the reader will appreciate the difficulties this presents to governments. It's all very well building sea walls and flood defences — citizens are likely to see the need for such measures and to welcome them. But the prospect of receiving huge numbers of 'climate refugees' from other nations is an entirely different matter.

At the moment we cannot be certain exactly how weather patterns will turn out if the world warms by two, three or four degrees. But there will inevitably be winners and losers, especially with regard to the critical aspect of food supply.

Nature's Adaptation

Nature too will be forced to adapt to a warming world. Some species will manage to adopt our human solution and to migrate. For others though, this may not be possible. Humanity faces a dilemma here. We have made quite a mess of things by introducing 'invasive species' in the past – sometimes deliberately, sometimes in error. Should we go on interfering in a similar manner by trying to move species to places where they will be safer from the effects of climate change? Alternatively, should we just leave it to nature to fend for herself? In which case, probably, many species will not make it, but others may thrive. Or, perhaps a mixture of these two approaches? We have many such dilemmas already, and no doubt many more will follow. I refer the reader back once more to those first weeks of lock-down that occurred in many countries at the start of the Coronavirus pandemic. As many of us witnessed at that time, left to her own devises, nature can spring back with an abundance that can surprise and amaze us.

Individual Adaptation

We've looked briefly above at what the individual might do in the case of sea-level rise, flood and food shortages. These are stark choices. For those who have the means to choose, the choice may have to be finding somewhere to live that is high enough to be out of harm's way, or otherwise to seek refuge in another region or another country. It's the severity of these choices that really brings home the importance of trying to tackle climate change now rather than have to face these awful choices at some point in the future.

A few points remain that have a direct bearing on an individual's circumstances.

Drought

We've noted above that drought is an increasing problem as a result of climate change. There are several reasons for this. An increasingly affluent population (and the increasing demands on agriculture) means that we have a greater requirement for water. Some areas rely on the melting of snow and ice in order to supply rivers, which in turn provide water to populations downstream. The final reason is most pertinent to our discussions here. Most rainfall gets 'wasted', so far as the human use of water is concerned. As we've seen above, the rain that falls in rural areas drains away quickly because of the lack of trees, and then floods low-lying areas downstream. Meanwhile, the rain that hits towns and cities runs off quickly into surface water drains, then it is taken away into rivers (where it may add to flooding) or into the sea. (Or sometimes the water may go into the foul sewer systems, so if there is a flood then things are even worse because of the dirtier and more polluted water.)

Even in places with quite high rainfall therefore, it is worth collecting water from roofs and storing it for later use in small gardens or for washing and flushing toilets. With some filtration (and/or boiling) it could be safe enough to drink. An underground tank could have a pump to raise water to a header tank that will then feed taps and appliances within a house or a business premises. The pump may be electric, or just a hand-operated pump. This is a relatively simple option, certainly suitable for the 'off-gridder', but also for the more conventional household or building.

Heatwaves

Although climate change means generally a warmer world, the disruption to weather patterns can cause severe cold as well as heatwaves. We've seen, in the last chapter, that insulation and having an alternative source of heat are good measures for saving energy and coping with any disruption to energy supply. We can also see these as adaptation measures for countries that might experience extreme cold events in the future.

It is the heatwave however that is likely to become the more common extreme weather event in the future — especially if average global temperature rise goes beyond two degrees. We can anticipate, at least for relatively wealthy countries, a steep rise in the use of air-conditioning. The energy used for this would unfortunately be contributing to the problem that it is trying to solve. And in high-density urban areas the heat displaced by cooling systems, coupled with the heat absorbed by buildings and hard surfaces just adds to the problems.

The traditional architecture of many Middle-Eastern and North African countries was developed to cope with high temperatures and we can still take a lot of lessons from them today. Simple measures such as narrow streets to provide shade, small windows, shutters on the sunlit areas of buildings, internal courtyards with fountains and passive ventilation systems can regulate temperature without having to resort to technology. Some areas can also benefit from using trees for shading and having a lot of nature around our buildings can also help to regulate temperature.

Different Pleasures

The modern home, at least in wealthy nations, is bristling with TV screens, computers, laptops, mobile phones, numerous household appliances, central heating and possibly air-conditioning. Outside, or in the garage, there may be two, three or four cars. The family will take several long car rides a week, either for work, to fetch supplies or for pleasure. They will likely go on holiday a few times a year, possibly by long-haul flights to other continents. This is the lifestyle to which many people aspire. They feel they have worked hard to obtain this level of comfort. Both adults in the household may be working full-time jobs with lengthy hours in order to maintain the level of income needed to finance this kind of life. The discussions about low-tech and off-grid housing in the earlier chapters will probably just seem absurd to such people. They might well feel that they would be ashamed to live in such a way.

If the reader has some concern for the planet then they may describe the high energy, fast-paced lifestyle as greedy, wasteful or irresponsible. As concerns over climate change and the related pressure on natural resources and loss of bio-diversity grow, then we are likely to all feel more guilty over our lifestyles, even whilst it is difficult to change.

Back in the Introduction we noted three broad categories or groupings of people that are relevant to our discussions — government, business and citizens (or consumers). Governments may have policies and initiate laws to tackle our problems. Businesses may well have an environmental ethic. As citizens, we may choose to try to influence government policy and the behaviour of businesses directly, through campaigning and activism, including protest. But as I have suggested in the Introduction, the biggest influence on both government and business is through the choices we make as consumers. So if we are to curtail the excesses of a high energy, high-tech, materialistic lifestyle, we need to think about what makes people aspire to such a life and how that might change.

The elements that make up an alternative lifestyle are sometimes described as 'simplicity'. The simple way of life might involve some or all of the following: Cooking food from scratch. A mainly vegetarian or vegan diet with locally-sourced food. Walking and cycling instead of driving. Repair and recycling. Cutting down or eliminating technology, especially phones and computers. Taking holidays locally. And also, incorporating some of the energy-saving and off-grid measures described in earlier chapters. There is a lot to be said for this way of life. In financial terms, the household described at the head of this chapter could perhaps live a simple lifestyle and only need to work two days a week on the same salary in order to meet their living costs. Then there would be plenty of time for walking, gardening, sports, art and craftwork, music, meeting with friends, slow cooking and all the other activities people say they are currently too busy to do. This is what I am describing as 'different pleasures' — it's all about those things that most people, at least in their more reflective moments, say they would love to do, if only they had the time! Could we convince people that this is a better way to live?

Well, first of all, it's no use preaching at people that their energy-intensive, materialistic lifestyle is trashing the planet. Most people are already aware of that by now, at least in part of their minds, but their hearts are currently telling them just to go on living to try to maximise their pleasure and show others how successful they are. Perhaps they rationalise this by saying they are trying to give their children the best possible start in life. Or that one person won't make a difference to the Earth's problems. Or that it's the government's job to fix things. Or China needs to change first. Or even that it is too late to save the planet so they might as well go on enjoying themselves whilst they still can. The simple lifestyle described above may well be mocked and ridiculed. The ridicule is the way that some people divert their own attention away from the need for change.

In this chapter, we're going a bit beyond what individuals and households might do to address the problems we face. We're asking what might be done to convince others of the need to change, and my contention here is that it's through different ways that we understand pleasure that change could be brought about.

So, I'd argue, one aspect of being a climate activist is to tackle this question of pleasure.

What then can the aspiring eco-warrior do to convince people, at this critical individual and personal level, that change would be a good thing? From the above, once again, the first message is surely not to preach to people on a personal level. (We can keep our political campaigning, activism or business ethic separate from our personal encounters with other folk.) Then secondly, if we believe in the simple lifestyle and the different pleasures it offers, we need to be living it ourselves — living the message. That way, people might just get curious and ask us how we seem to always be relaxed and happy whilst apparently doing very little work! We will then have earned the right to speak and can describe how we've gone about changing our own lives, but still without voicing any condemnation of others.

We also need to keep in mind that people usually make changes for personal reasons rather than because of their commitment to a cause or an ideology. Whilst we might say that we are adopting a simple lifestyle for the sake of the planet, actually it might more likely be because we find the constant bleeping, clicking and sheer stupidity of modern gadgets just really irritating! Or because we would actually rather spend time walking, swimming, camping or doing artwork, music or writing for the shear pleasure of these activities and not waste our life in a boring job just to make money. So it is a bit disingenuous to describe the high-earning, high energy, high-tech family as selfish or profligate whilst we are in our ivory tower of pious and self-righteous 'sustainability'. Actually, whilst there are certainly some greedy and selfish people, we are all self-serving and we all have an image of ourselves as 'doing the right thing' individually and for our children. It's just that the simple lifestyle is the one that offers us a long-term hope for the future. So let's not give the suggestion that simplicity is the more 'moral' choice. Everyone's choices could be described as 'moral' or 'selfish' depending on the perspective.

And this is not to disparage 'stuff' in general. Arts and crafts, along with beautiful buildings and gardens are still stuff. We are surely right to lavish care and attention on these as part of human culture as well as just for sheer pleasure. But our relationship with stuff — whether the high-tech gadget, the mass-produced product or the hand-crafted artefact — is complex. So again, moralising too much can distract us.

It's certainly difficult to change suddenly. The prospect of a greatly reduced income can seem daunting and likewise the thought of living without a mobile phone or a laptop close at hand can feel like losing our identity! But once a few changes have been accomplished, then further steps get easier. Paradoxical as it may seem, it's often the case that we have fewer money worries when we have less money. And we can have more meaningful contact with others when there is only limited time given over to social media, text or email.

One way to initiate change is to adopt what I describe as the 'stay-in-bed' approach to tackling climate change. I'm not exactly sure where I have got this phrase from, but the general idea may be attributed to Tom Hodgkinson, editor of *The Idler* magazine. The idea is that as things break down or wear out, don't bother to replace them. If they can be repaired, then yes, go with the repair. But if, as a householder or a business, life can go on without whatever it is that's broken, then all the better. That way, before too long, the car will be gone, then the TV, then the lawn mower, and so on. The benefit of this approach is that some people (men especially) can be obsessed with gadgets. As such, when they 'go green', it means to them that they just replace one set of gadgets for another. Even if energy consumption is thereby reduced, there is still a lot of stuff being produced and the materialistic mindset is not really tackled at all. Letting things wear out, on the other hand, allows for a much healthier attitude to stuff, and I think this in turn can lead to the broader values of simplicity that I have tried to outline above.

The 'stay-in-bed' strategy leads us into another way of looking at things — sorting out what are our true priorities. That way, it's easier to let go of the things that break or that we just never use or are in the way and to focus instead on what's truly important to us. A person might find most satisfaction through their work — it is a vocation for them, not just a job — so they will willingly make sacrifices to follow their career. Or it may be the pursuit of art or music, which has up until now been more of a hobby than a vocation. When speaking to others on a personal level, this is a great approach. We can ask: What really floats their boat? What would they do if money was no object and they need not work for a living? Then we can encourage people to follow that dream with all their energy! Thus, we are meeting people — as I've suggested above — at the level of their deepest pleasures, rather than trying to convince them for moral reasons. This is a very positive message to offer people, as opposed to criticising their lifestyle and making uninvited suggestions about how they might change!

Over time, trying to focus on what's really important to us will lead to long-term rather than short-term thinking. And that is when we start to align with the concerns of the planet that I have been describing in this book. In the broadest of perspectives, tackling climate change, resource depletion and bio-diversity loss is long-term thinking.

The reader may object at this point, by saying that an individual's life ambition may be to become a billionaire via the oil industry or some such counter-example, and therefore suggesting to them that they 'follow their dream' is actually a terrible idea! The criticism is accepted. But in turn I point out that if someone's life goal is so demonstrably bad then no argument is likely to dissuade them anyway — we might as well just wish them luck in their endeavours! Challenging their ambition is likely to make them even more determined to do what we find objectionable.

The reader might further object that even if someone's goals in life are relatively benign, then still, waiting for them to come around to long-term thinking and recognising how this fits in with the concerns of the planet might be a very long wait indeed! In fact, that day may never come. I suggest however that an encounter where we discuss our dreams and aspirations for life is worthwhile in and of itself. It builds trust, which may allow us to share our own visions for the future. This is much better than launching into trying to persuade someone to switch to an electric car or replace their gas boiler with a heat pump!

In summary then, the would-be eco-warrior is best to lead by example and be genuinely happy in their chosen lifestyle before saying anything that might be about trying to get folk to change. Above all else, the danger is to come across as pious and self-righteous! If someone is thinking that humanity is hopelessly lost, greedy and stupid, then that attitude is likely to show through, and our words and manner will condemn us. If, on the other hand, we really believe that most people are full of potential, trying to do their best and generally keen on fairness, kindness, loyalty and looking after their families, then we will have a good start at engaging with people. Provided we have this attitude then talking about people's dreams and aspirations is going to bring out the best in people. In short, it's a personal approach rather than trying to present people with objective arguments, or worse, moral pronouncements. And it helps to be very clear in our own minds whether we like people and think that humanity is worthwhile! If not, then anything we might do is likely to appear disingenuous.

Polity

The last chapter focused on our personal relations with people and our shared interests in pleasure and trying to realise our goals in life. I've suggested in this book that it's the personal life of citizens that is the real driver for change. If we, as citizens, live in different ways then business and government will wake up and change their ways in turn. Otherwise the politician will not get re-elected and the manufacturer's products will remain on the shelves.

In the last chapter I've said that campaigning and activism are ways that we might try to influence government and business directly. In this chapter, I want to deal briefly with a further alternative. Instead of just waiting for politicians to catch up, could we change the way we govern ourselves and thereby bring about new laws and regulations to tackle climate change and address our problems more quickly? The activist group Extinction Rebellion, amongst others, has suggested 'citizens' assemblies'. This involves choosing a group of citizens by lot, who then come together to deliberate a particular topic. If, for instance, assemblies were set up to discuss climate change, they might arrive at solutions that have come from the grass roots of people's lives. The government would then be obliged to implement the decisions reached (or at least, this is the hope). Or it may be that normal government is superseded altogether and we just have the assemblies.

Would this be better, or worse?

Well, critics of such proposals might suggest that citizens are more interested in their own personal well-being and less interested in the long-term benefit and protection of society at large. They would argue that people are not good enough for this type of democracy and that we would be better sticking with the current system. For all its faults, such folk might argue, representative democracy at least takes some account of society at large and the protection of the planet.

Proponents of citizens' assemblies, on the other hand, suggest that once ordinary people are given the opportunity to take some time to think seriously about a particular issue, they show remarkable foresight and wisdom.

Who is right?

It would be good to at least give citizens' assemblies a go — and there have been experiments in many countries that have shown encouraging results. We could counter the critics by saying that rather than people not being good enough for this type of decision-making, we are just not attuned to it. But I think this is changing. The ways groups organise themselves these days show a lot of the qualities of genuine shared decision-making — making sure everyone is heard, giving everyone an equal say, openness, tolerance, acceptance, accountability — these are the subtle (and sometimes not so subtle) shifts from the old style of top-down governance.

Even if big government does not undergo such a radical shift, the methods of shared decision-making are being practised in campaigning and activist groups. So these changes are being embedded in us and I believe they are positive steps for the future.

Therefore, as well as activism that is aimed directly at solving climate change, resource depletion and loss of bio-diversity, an activism that aims at political change is also a worthwhile strategy. It is less direct, certainly, but the wider changes that a more deliberative form of democracy could bring about are very significant. Social justice, climate change, bio-diversity, resources, capitalism and democracy are all inextricably linked.

Dystopia?

I've tried to focus on the small-scale and the practical in this book. The problems that face us can seem vast, and also often remote and abstract. We might respond by switching off, or feeling despair. Young people today are often landed with the task of having to save the planet, because of the way the issues are presented to us. This is an intolerable burden. It is no wonder that there can often be a sense of hopelessness. And the stories of the future we are given — in novels, films and TV — are often dystopian visions. Are we really heading for a collapse in civilisation, where conditions on Earth are so bad that only a small remnant of humanity survives — maybe in Greenland, or Antarctica — and perhaps another remnant has set up on Mars or the Moon? That's often the ultimatum presented to us by a lot of otherwise well-meaning activists and climate experts, and also, as I've said above, by our novelists and film-makers.

So in this chapter I want to ask, how likely is it that such a dystopia will come about?

Earlier in the book, I've described the main mitigation and adaptation measures we could take. We are well behind in our mitigation measures, but there is still at least a few years left when mitigation alone would be enough to turn things around. After the next few years though, if we don't do enough on the mitigation front, we will have reached a tipping point where the climate is changing so rapidly because of nature that it is essentially out of control. Then our focus would have to be mainly on adaptation.

The critical question for us then would be, how much will the climate change, just by natural processes, before it settles down into a new stable state? And that question leads us to ask how much adaptation we would need to make in order to be able to live in the new stable state?

(I'm ignoring here the benefits, or otherwise, of implementing one or more of the geo-engineering measures described earlier in the book. I'm sceptical about these ever being tried out on a large enough scale to make much of a difference to the basic mitigation/adaptation discussion presented in earlier chapters.)

How much then would the climate change if we largely fail in our mitigation efforts? The science seems to suggest anywhere between around four and six degrees above pre-industrial levels, although as more research takes place, the figures vary. How much adaptation would it take for humans to go on living reasonably okay in such a world? Well, it has to be said, a huge amount of adaptation! But is it possible? Certainly, yes! The difference between mitigation and adaptation (and the reason I have emphasised these terms so much in the book) is the different mindsets they each involve. Mitigation is to try to ward off a problem that might, to our immediate senses, just never happen. With adaptation, we can already see the problems — the storms, droughts and heatwaves — and so we know it is time to roll up our sleeves and get on with the work that needs to be done.

The other big thing to say about dystopian visions of the future is simply that we need to replace them with alternative visions. Our story-tellers need to show us ways we can live happily on an Earth potentially very different from the one we have known up until now. That way, they will not be confronting people with an ultimatum — change your ways or this is your fate! Instead we'll see that all that is good in humanity can be protected and nourished. There is a new genre of fiction emerging called 'solar punk', which takes up this vision. (The term 'solar punk' is coined in opposition to 'cyber punk', which usually involves dystopian high-tech futures.)

This brings us to our final chapter. Hope!

,

Hope

Sometimes an argument is presented to us that says ordinary people have no choice but to live unsustainably because of their political or economic circumstances. For instance, it is said that even a homeless person in the United States has a higher carbon footprint than the Earth could sustain (largely because of the energy use of night shelters, soup kitchens, medical facilities, etc.). Or, the peasant farmer in many countries has no choice but to fell ancient forest and plant cash crops for the consumption of richer nations. Or the farmer in a wealthy nation has no choice but to use pesticides, artificial fertilisers and large amounts of machinery, otherwise they simply could not continue farming. But whilst I don't for a moment want to detract from the difficulties of such scenarios, and hundreds more like them, I don't think the problems are insurmountable. The argument goes that situations such as the ones I have described above require 'structural' change in order to be solved. In other words, big politics, legislation, and perhaps funding, taxation, and trade agreements, such that individuals are not 'compelled' to make a living in such a way that the climate and environment suffer. But we can see that often this does not work, even where governments make substantial efforts to implement the structural changes I've described.

Instead, I think that hope lies with individuals, families and small communities. That has been my focus in this book. I think we are already waking up to the need for action, and many folk are already wide awake! And I think the hope on offer is not a burden to us. The changes I have described earlier in the book could be summarised as, 'slow down', 'keep things simple' and 'stay local'. All of that is immediately within our grasp — it does not rely on action by government, or buying a lot of renewable gadgets. The benefits are the 'different pleasures' I have described — less need to spend long hours just trying to make a living — therefore, more time to do the stuff that really interests us, be it sport, crafts, music, writing, or just being with friends and family. More time and space for nature. More time, and good reasons, to cook meals slowly from scratch. Even time to build our own houses and grow some of our own food. All of the above can also be part of building resilient communities that could self-organise, should the need arise, because of severe weather events or other disruptions in the future. We would no longer have a precarious set of individuals, totally reliant on the state and the massive infrastructures of global communications and supply chains. We could have communities that can self-govern and who could take great pride and pleasure in their autonomy. That would be a world that is truly rich!

So the problems we face now are not just

annoying issues that we need to get out of the way so that we can get back to working 50 hours a week, spending many more hours in traffic jams, eating junk food, never speaking to our neighbours and being too tired to do any of the stuff that we really want to do, because we have to pay for all the stuff that allows us to work the 50 hours a week... And so on, around and around. Is this any way to live, even if we did stop climate change and all the other problems? No. Instead those problems are a wake-up call to a much more radical change and a much more radical hope! I'm closing now with this message of hope. The changes we need to make are possible and within our power. Let's be that radical change!

Review of Author's Main Works

Conatus

It's difficult to have any certainty over truth, so we must improvise with stories.

Many of the stories we tell about the world involve splitting it up. This can lead us into contradictions.

Seeing the world as just 'The One' — 'Not Two', an undivided whole — is however equally problematic. It leads into all the paradoxes that seem to surface when we talk about eternity and infinity.

The process of truth-seeking that we follow today is to start from observation. We then follow through to basing our ethics and ideals on how people actually behave, and our theories of aesthetics on what people actually like — rather than seeking a source for ethics and aesthetics elsewhere.

However, this process of truth-seeking — starting from observation — whilst it may seem to be logical, actually still gets things wrong. The reason is that 'observation' occurs much later than is generally considered in our experience of the world.

It is 'sensation' that is primary — and this involves emotions as well as information from the senses. 'Perception' follows from this — we might better term it 'awareness'. And then a lot of actions (including acts that we would term

71

'moral') follow on immediately from this — 'impulse'. It is only at the next stage — 'image' — that we have anything close to what is described as observation. To have an image is to be aware of our awareness, and it already includes a lot of inner interpretation of what we have experienced with our emotions and our senses. This we never truly 'observe' — we always bring pre-conscious notions to our truth-seeking, along with rationalisations of what we've already done or wanted to do at the 'impulse' stage.

There is a further method of truth-seeking that we might call 'top-down' rather than bottom-up. This (and avoiding any religious interpretation of it) is to suggest that there are higher orders of being, and these higher orders have an influence on our lives.

To avoid any 'mysterian' interpretation of this, we can consider Aristotle's understanding of 'the soul'. For him, the soul is just the sum of the mind and body's actions in the world. Applying this same principle to other orders of being, we can recognise, in plain language, culture, eco-systems, the bio-sphere, the life within the solar system, the galaxy and the universe as a whole, all to be 'higher orders'.

In Conatus, it is contested that all these levels have emergent properties and have some kind of 'downward causation'. They affect us!

Putting the above thoughts together, the book concludes that the influences that impact on us come from 'below' — as sensation, perception, impulse, image and symbol — and from 'above'

— universe, galaxy, solar system, bio-sphere, eco-system, and our way of being in the world for our minds and bodies.

From our perspective — value is innate. Values come before ethics and morality — so too does a sense of the sacredness of nature, including our own human nature. One way to look at this is to say that all this stems from the beauty gifted to us by the cosmos.

From all of the above, a virtuous life is best expressed through a life of simplicity, where the main elements are compassion, humility and a sense of awe and reverence towards nature and the wider cosmos.

Twenty-One Levels of Self-Deception

There is an individual desire for pleasure — there is also the social concern for the 'common good'. The book's initial question is whether these two may be in conflict.

One way the book addresses this question is through the contrast of 'ascendancy' and 'descendancy' — with ascendancy being identified with spirit (in the broadest sense of the word) and descendancy being associated with soul.

We are not 'mortals' — born out of nothing and heading for nothing — we are 'natals' — born to become.

The book suggests that nurture of the soul (and the book recognises a philosophical rather than a religious view of the soul here — the combination of mind, body and our manner of being in the world) leads us towards better results. The aspirations of spirit are ultimately unrealisable.

There are three things that the book identifies as being of particular relevance in relation to descendancy (the soul):

1. We need to know ourselves as we actually are — in particular, we need to strip away 'false selves' and false notions of the self. We can practice 'letting go' to rid ourselves of our false selves.
2. We need to be clear about where our true pleasures lie.
3. We need to recognise the sacredness of nature — including human nature and including our own personal human nature.

Beauty is our surest guide we have to navigating all of this — but beauty understood here to include the paradox of wild nature, where there is predator and prey as well as benign co-operation. And beauty also includes human wild propensities towards evil as well as good. Beauty — in this sense — is our first value. From beauty, all other values spring.

Values though can be conflicted and so should be seen as a conversation, and not as a set of ideals.

Initially, it seems that, even if an individual life is seen as primarily about pleasure, the desire for pleasure and the desire to help the common good can be seen as one and the same. But the work suggests that there is more going on. Rather than just an exchange of pleasures, we become beauty and pleasure, and this is our gift back to the world.

In all of this, the book makes clear that we give of ourselves because the universe has first gifted to us — this is grace.

Utopia, Governance and the Commons

Ideas about community and small-scale 'participatory' politics are great in theory, but most of us are just not of the right mindset to make these work in practice.

One solution is to have strong and competent leaders.

A more difficult — although potentially better — solution is for us to change as people.

A large part — and somewhat unexpected part — of the change needed is for us to realise a sense of enchantment.

This means seeing the beauty of the world and in other people in a specific way. It means recognising where our own pleasures lie, and potentially, 'following our bliss'. It means following what we might start to see as our 'life-work' with a single-minded determination.

Apart from recognising where our true pleasure lies the other issue that holds us back from being the kind of people who could affect real political change is our power relations. We need to be 'power-under'.

It's the conclusion of the book that the changes we need for a viable utopia are: To know our own pleasure, follow our bliss, focus on our life work, and to see all this within the context of a power-under approach to life.

Dreamtree

There are no real splits in the world.

The kingdom of heaven is within you.

Who we really are as people is expressed mainly through what we find pleasurable.

Pleasure can be through shared pleasure. Pleasure can also be as an 'exchange of gifts'. Pleasure is a two-way street, always as an interaction with society, culture, nature, the eco-system.

The reason why pleasure works as gift-giving is because the universe has started off the gift exchange process for each of us by giving us life and the various beautiful aspects of our minds, our bodies and our ways of being in the world.

This explanation of gift-giving — as a response to the grace given to us by the universe — is a myth. By that I don't mean it is untrue — just that it is a story that might help us to make sense of the world. But if it doesn't help then leave it. This use of myth helps us to avoid insisting on some kind of absolute truth, and potentially avoids a lot of argument that might otherwise ensue!